What Can We Make?

John Prater

CAMBRIDGE
UNIVERSITY PRESS

"What can we make?" said Bear.

"Let's make
a robot," said
Hedgehog.

3

Hedgehog made the robot's body.

Bear made the robot's head.

Hedgehog made the robot's arms.

"Here's the head," said Bear.

"Let's paint a mouth," said
Hedgehog.

Bear went to get some paint.

Bear painted the robot's mouth.

"Hello," said the robot.

"It was me!" said Hedgehog.